PRAISE FOR *CHECKMATE!*

"Just as you win at chess by knowing the rules and thinking ahead, *Checkmate* provides the reader with a foundation and planning format for what it takes to win in the marketplace. Practical and useful coaching advice for anyone who wants to move to the next level in their business or organization."

—Constantino Salios
The Barnabas Group

CHECKMATE!

CHECKMATE!

Winning Tactics for Translating Ideas into Money

John Whitt

Published in the United States by Redwood Publishing, LLC.

Books are available at special discounts when purchased in bulk for sales promotions or corporate use. For more information, please write: **info@redwooddigitalpublishing.com** and include the title of the book in the email subject line.

Printed in the United States of America

To contact the author:
John Whitt
www.businesswhitt.com
info@redwooddigitalpublishing.com

Paperback ISBN: 978-1-947341-97-5
eBook ISBN: 978-1-947341-96-8

Library of Congress Control Number: 2016937090

Cover Design: Jane Korunoski
Interior Design: Ghislain Viau

To my wife, the lovely Mrs. Tracy whose love, support,
and encouragement kept the process going.

ACKNOWLEDGMENTS

I'd like to thank to my son, Johnny, whose work behind the camera allowed ideas like this book to come to fruition.

And, a very special thanks to Georgia Perkey for her knowledge and expertise, and for providing insight on the foundational ideas in the book.

CONTENTS

FOREWORD

CHECKMATE – THE ULTIMATE VICTORY IN THE STRATEGIC game of chess, a timeless competition dating back to the 6th century.

Coach John Whitt has combined the strategic thought process he developed playing competitive chess with his multi decade business experience in project management and business coaching to deliver a proven process that will help business owners convert their ideas into revenue.

Checkmate is an easy to read, easy to follow introduction into the practical application of proven business principles and five key attributes for success Whitt has created and refined as essential for business to thrive.

No matter where you or your business are on the business life cycle *Checkmate* is a must read. I know readers will enjoy the content and encourage you to apply its principles to your business and life. Enjoy!

Robert Hechler
President – Business Coaching of Southern California

INTRODUCTION

I'M JOHN WHITT AND I'VE BEEN IN THE COACHING PRACTICE, one way or another, for the past sixteen years. For the last six years, I've been associated with the FocalPoint Coaching Team powered by Brian Tracy. Brian Tracy is a noted author, public speaker, and one of the originals in the world of business coaching and publishing.

I work with business owners, executives, and sales professionals every day to make the right moves for their business. It's all about results. When you make the right moves you achieve better results. My clients are looking for results that will provide the time and financial freedom to live the life they want to live for themselves and their families. And when they are fortunate and make more than they need, they can and will make a contribution to the less fortunate.

We all have challenges in life and I feel I've had my share. I thank the relationship I developed late in life with Jesus for giving me the wisdom and the guidance to stay the course and continue in his good works. I love what I do, but I would be truly remiss if I failed to mention the Bible and my faith as the ultimate driving force for this effort. I feel compelled to share the knowledge I've gained as a responsibility to help others achieve more and give more. Later on I'll share a story that outlines why I've chosen to outline a simple process for translating ideas into money or whatever result you desire. When you have money though, "amazing" happens much easier.

My two major passions outside of business are chess and golf. I learned to play competitive chess in high school. Today I play chess online for fun, but my strategic thinking process was shaped in part by my competitive chess days. With golf, I play to clear my head and enjoy an afternoon away from the hustle and bustle of the everyday world. Some people think golf is too hard and too frustrating. They don't play because they are just not certain whether they are going to play well and enjoy the time. Uncertainty and frustration are also huge fears for business owners and those that are considering owning and operating their own business. Who wants to spend their time frustrated and anxious? However, in both golf and chess, if we focus more on the process than the outcome, there is less frustration and less anxiety. Once again, in business the key is to focus on the process.

My thirty-year corporate career has been all about project creation and management. I started out as an architect and moved into construction, and then transitioned to designing and coordinating large-enterprise technology projects. At one point my project management business had over 1,500 projects running simultaneously, totaling over 500 million dollars in construction costs. At that point I transitioned my project skill set from construction to technology because, not only did we have to construct the buildings, but we also had to keep track of them … thousands of them! There were no widespread platforms for tracking at that time. Creating a technology platform was the solution to providing thousands of employees access to the data they needed on thousands of properties. Big crazy projects like these—it's what I do.

So there you have it! I'm a chess player and a golfer who looks at life like a project. Every project has a starting point and a goal. I work with people to identify a strategy and a plan to get from wherever they are to wherever they want to go. Point A to Point B—it's that simple!

Let's get started!

TRANSLATING IDEAS
INTO MONEY

WELCOME TO BUSINESS WHITT.

You already know a little bit about me, but here's a quick recap—I'm a business coach, video show host for BusinessWhitt's Better Business Results, and creator of the *Make the Right Moves* coaching forum.

And now, an author. I am taking what I've learned over the years—strategic thinking, managing projects, and coaching —and I've created a simple how-to book for translating ideas into money.

After reading the materials presented here, it is my hope that you understand my one belief—wherever you are and whatever you're doing, you will achieve more success and greater results by making the right moves in your business, in the right order and at the right time. While this information mainly applies to business, the strategies can be used for personal or professional projects.

Now, I'm sure you're wondering—what is BusinessWhitt?

Aside from being a pun with my last name, BusinessWhitt embodies the definition of the word wit. Wit is defined in the dictionary in two ways, both of which are at the core of the BusinessWhitt brand promise.

> **wit**[1] *noun*
>
> **1.** mental sharpness and inventiveness; keen intelligence. *"he does not lack perception or native wit"*
> synonyms: intelligence, shrewdness, astuteness, cleverness, canniness, sense, common sense, wisdom, sagacity, judgment, acumen, insight;
> **2.** a natural aptitude for using words and ideas in a quick and inventive way to create humor. *"a player with a sharp tongue and a quick wit"*
> synonyms: wittiness, humor, funniness, drollery, esprit; repartee, badinage, banter, wordplay; jokes, witticisms, quips, puns

The best business builders all display a keen intelligence when it comes to growing their organizations. And it isn't so much about them just knowing "what" to do, rather they possess an identifiable depth of insight that leverages the "why" and "when" certain success strategies are to be executed.

Where did this intelligence come from? Bottom line, it was learned. Unfortunately too many small business owners struggle along and all too often they figure out the right moves they should have made a little too late. BusinessWhitt is committed to breaking this pattern by infusing small business owners with business-building *wit* so that they learn the right moves to make, in the right order, and increase their chances of winning. This passion and mission to help others make the right moves in their business is what inspired our logo.

by John Whitt

The chess pawn structure in the BusinessWhitt logo represents the foundation of the business-building battle. They represent the basic day-in and day-out blocking and tackling moves that must occur in every business to support success. Stay firm in this foundation and focus on learning and executing the right moves and success grows closer. Make the wrong moves and the distance to reach desired goals increases. There's no two ways about it; business success requires business wit.

Having the wit to build a business is imperative and of course we have a terrific respect for intelligence. But interestingly enough, it's actually the second definition of wit that separates the best from the rest. Sure, we would all prefer not to make mistakes and have our plans execute perfectly, however perfection isn't possible. Even the best laid plans come unraveled through unexpected turns. And this is why we believe that a sense of humor is paramount when it comes to overcoming adversity. We know that more is learned by failure than success, and looking at life's blunders with a sense of humor keeps stress down, creativity high, and drives us to fight for our goal yet another day. We don't choose when problems or issues occur. Our choice is in our response. We choose to have it be a beautiful response.

Now, if I asked you why you started your business, what would your response be?

I'm guessing you've said something like, "I thought I had a great idea and I wanted to turn it into money." Or, "I was passionate about my hobby and I want to make money doing what I love." But having a good idea isn't the only thing you need. You need to be able to translate your ideas into money.

First, let me state one thing—ideas are IMPERATIVE!! Ideas and innovation fuel the economy and makes our lives better. However, ideas are just that (things floating around in the air) unless followed up with execution. You will hear this more than once, so get used to it! The reality is that we need to know how to execute on our plans and ideas in order to make those ideas turn into results.

As a business coach you would not believe how many good ideas I hear from my clients. It's pretty amazing. And at one point during our time together, I'll hear lots of them say this common statement: "It's all in the execution." Yet the biggest hang-up that I see with almost everyone I coach *by far*, is their lack of execution on the ideas they have. And the most concerning part of it all is that their really good ideas eventually die because they don't get executed.

Opportunities (and results) that could have bubbled up to the surface through a great idea remain buried and unrealized. Think about it—how many amazing ideas have you personally had that you never executed? Even worse—how many were actually executed by someone else? And as you're watching their success unfold, all you have left to say is, "Hey, I thought of that." Ouch. Not a good feeling, right?

The most amazing example on this topic is Nokia. More than seven years before Apple rolled out the iPhone, the Nokia team showed a phone with a color touch-screen set above a single button. The device was shown locating a restaurant, playing a racing game and ordering lipstick. In the late 1990s, Nokia secretly developed another alluring product: a tablet computer with a wireless connection and touch screen—all features today of the hot-selling Apple iPad.

"Oh, my God," Mr Nuovo says as he clicks through his old slides. "We had it completely nailed."

Consumers never saw either device. The gadgets were casualties of a corporate culture that lavished funds on research but squandered opportunities to bring the innovations it produced to market.

There are a lot of reasons why people don't execute their ideas, but among the variety and uniqueness of individuals whom I coach, there is one main thing I've noticed that haunts them all and keeps them from tasting the fruit of their good ideas. When starting up any coaching activity, I see the same pattern from all of my clients. I call it "judgement mode." Let me explain.

My role is *not* to tell others what to do.

My role is to help enable others to come to conclusions and decisions that will be effective for their business.

So rather than tell someone an idea, or something they should do, I might say "Have you considered this idea?" or "What do you think of this idea?"

What I'm really doing is trying to plant the seed of thought. But, when I start asking these questions, everyone, and I mean everyone, goes into "judgement mode" when I ask these questions. They quickly evaluate the idea and judge the result they *think* they will get from past behaviors and results. If it fits in with successful behaviors and executions from the past, it is an approved idea. If it fits with past failures, it gets rejected. And if it is an unknown, the owner begins thinking about the idea, convinced that there's a likelihood it will fail. Don't get me wrong—the idea of going down an unknown path and failing *is* scary. If I stopped at this, then the conversation (either with me or with themselves) turns into idea/judge, idea/judge, idea/judge and so on. The fallacy here is that people judge their future successes based on their past actions and results. They rarely think about whether their past actions were correct and/or valid. So, they often let the results of the past hold them back from a different and potentially better future.

Let me illustrate this with a story.

One of my first clients had this issue with judging success based on past actions and results, in a bad way. Unfortunately it had led him to near bankruptcy. He reached out to me as a last resort. He told me that he had tried everything he knew and could think of, to stop his business from spiraling downward to oblivion, without success. When we began our discussion, I asked him what *he* thought *he* needed to do to turn his business around. He replied that he had no ideas left. So I began to suggest some options. In particular, I suggested that he open up new markets. His market—residential real estate—dried up almost overnight with the Great Recession. However, he quickly rejected each option I suggested. Often he said something like "That's impossible!" or "I can't do that." He came up with all kinds of reasons why every one of my suggested ideas would fail. He just could not see his way out of the dark. After a few of these "judgement" situations, I switched tactics and asked him if he knew for a fact that these opportunities would fail. He had to admit that it was his opinion that they would fail. I then asked him if other companies like his had successfully serviced the new markets we were discussing and he said that he didn't know of any specific company. But, he did admit that he thought *some* company out there had to be providing his service to those markets. Ah ha! So, now it was a possibility. I then said, "If they can do it, so can you."

The issue was that he simply didn't know *HOW* to do it, and because he didn't know, how he couldn't imagine doing it for himself. I shared with him that knowing how was something we could figure out. That if someone else could do it, we could certainly figure it out and that learning how was a process with which I was very familiar. Once we took the "how" out of the idea process we began to consider many more ideas. We ultimately reached several good decisions that ended up increasing his business 372% in the next ten months! Yes, it was touch and go in the beginning. Without removing the implementation activity from the decision we may have never come up with a solution.

This isn't an unusual situation. In fact, it has occurred with every single coaching client with whom I have worked. Some more and some less but none are immune. It takes practice to not let past events dictate future results. But the sweet satisfaction of success makes the practice oh so worthwhile.

It's stories and experiences like this that fuel my passion to help small business owners gain clarity and achieve success faster, more consistently and more predictably. Your business success is out there and ready for the taking. I want to help you make it a reality.

I hope to accomplish two objectives with this book:

1. I'd like you to be free of the "how" when you're creating new ideas and opportunities for your business success. Let the processes in this manual be the how. Let your ideas of the future be free of your past restrictions and results.

2. I'd like the processes in this manual be your GO TO resource for when you start a new project. The tools in this book will self select the best ideas and the best results from your ideas. I promise—the processes aren't difficult. Execution takes practice so refer to the manual often. If you use the tools in the manual when beginning your project, you'll be significantly more successful in your execution and you'll reduce the cost of any idea or project.

Next up, I want you to identify some goals so that you can keep them in mind as you read through the book. Following our Goals discussion is an "objectives" section which will give you the HOW.

The goals are **WHAT** you're looking to accomplish and your objectives are **HOW** you'll accomplish them.

GOALS

"Without Goals we are lost."
—Brian Tracy

TAKE OUT A SHEET OF PAPER AND SPEND A COUPLE OF minutes to quickly jot down the goals you'd like to accomplish after having read this book. Next ask yourself *why*. WHY do you want to learn the tactical steps, the process for translating ideas into money? Take a couple of minutes and identify WHY this is so important. What does this mean to you? Your business? Your family. Your employees. Your friends. What will you do with the results? Your why is critical to overcoming the adversity that occurs with change. After you've identified your why, identify an idea that you have worked on, or are working on, then follow the process outlined in the pages of this book. You will digest the information and gain greater clarity by practicing the material immediately rather than waiting and going through it again.

If you have completed the strategic questionnaire from our Make the Right Moves Coaching forum (visit my website, link below) you might have already identified some of your key ideas. It's ok if you haven't.

You can do it later. Even so, jot down a quick list of the ideas you want to implement. Let this be a working draft.

http://maketherightmovesbusinesscoaching.com/checkmateworksheets

> *There is no guarantee of reaching a goal at a certain time, there is a guarantee of never attaining goals that are never set.*
>
> —David McNally

_____

_____

_____

_____

_____

_____

_____

_____

_____

_____

_____

_____

_____

_____

_____

_____

_____

_____

OBJECTIVES

"Management by objective works— if you know the objectives. Ninety percent of the time, you don't."
—Peter Drucker

ALRIGHT, YOU HAVE YOUR "WHAT." DON'T LOSE THAT PAPER. These are your goals! Fold it up, put it inside the book, and review it as you read through each section in the rest of this material.

Now, the "how." So, let's talk about objectives. Ideas and innovations are great but they go nowhere without intentional execution. Execution takes an idea and turns it into money.

The remainder of this book will provide you with information how to turn your "what" goals into results and an action plan for success. It is up to you to use the information and take action. Your ability to take action will reap success. Without effort, you can't expect results.

There are **five key attributes** required for success and each will be individually defined a bit later. First we need to define the **method for placing your "X."** Your "X" is a definition of what actions you need to execute to translate your idea(s) into money. These are the "moves" you need to make. As noted earlier, when you identify and make the right moves, success and results occur much faster.

Brian Tracy first told a similar story of "X" in his book, *Focal Point*. The story of "X" goes like this:

> NASA is launching a rocket. It is on the launch pad in countdown mode…20-19-18-17. An engineer exclaims, "Stop! It's not working. We need to cancel the launch." The launch is scrapped and the engineers go back to work. Six months later, they try again. The same problem occurs and the launch is cancelled.
>
> The frustrated engineers reach out to the foremost rocket scientist in the world. He agrees to help and visits the project site to examine the rocket. After a long period of time, he takes a big, black felt marker out and places an X on the rocket's dial. He says, "This is your problem right here! Fix this dial and everything will work just fine." The engineers are happy and excited. They fix the rocket as prescribed by the scientist and when they are ready to launch, it works!
>
> In the meantime the scientist has submitted an invoice to NASA for his work. The NASA administrator looks at it and says, "$10,000? You were only here for a half hour!" The scientist asks the administrator if he would like him to revise the invoice and the administrator happily responds affirmatively, thanking the scientist for the revision.
>
> The following week the administrator receives another invoice from the rocket scientist. The new invoice stated:
>
> – Value of time to put the X on the rocket
>   dial $1
>
> – Value of time to know on which dial to put
>   the X $9,999

This anecdote is synonymous with how you can get the most out of this book. You must understand where your "X" is. It's the single most important thing for you to know about your business and this is where we will spend our time determining what is effective, what is important, and what action(s) you need to take. Focus on the "X" and you Make the Right Moves for your business. I'll help you delve into your projects and give you the details so that you understand what you are looking for and where that "X" is for translating your ideas into money.

Italian astronomer Galileo said, "You cannot teach a man anything; you can only help him to find it within himself."

The truth and reality is that YOU must take charge so that YOU can make something happen.

Which leads me to the last consideration before we get into the five key attributes—your attitude and the learning process. Simply put, you need the right attitude to start this and be able to successfully move through the process. If you don't have that, you will never truly be able to start the process.

Note to reader: At the end of each of the Key Attributes chapters, you'll find a reference to worksheets that will help you work through that particular attribute. You will be able to view all the worksheets in a sample format on my website, which shows you how each can be applied to projects. You will then be able to purchase and download those worksheets, as blank fillable PDFs, to save you time in lieu of creating your own worksheets. You could then take the worksheets and fill them out for your own needs.

YOUR ATTITUDE & LEARNING

BEFORE WE GET STARTED, YOU HAVE TO BE SURE THAT YOU have a positive outlook on your project and you are ready to learn.

Beliefs and attitudes can make or break us. A positive, growth mindset generally yields positive results. A negative mindset can stunt growth and development. All projects encounter a variety of challenges, both known and unknown. If you have a mindset of perseverance and the belief that you can solve the problem, you stand a much better chance of successfully navigating through the challenging moments on your journey to success.

Everything rises and falls on attitude and attitude drives behavior. If you think you can or can't you're probably right! If you think you can you will. If you think you can't you won't. Visit my checkmate videos site (link below) to view an extended Taking Responsibility video presentation.

http://maketherightmovesbusinesscoaching.com/checkmatevideos/

Determining the kind of attitude you possess means taking a look at your responses to problems or challenges that arise.

Are you proactive? Do you take ownership? Or do you place blame? Take a look at the graphic below. Are you an "above the line" or a "below the line" type of person? You're invited to visit the checkmate videos site (link below) to view a video presentation of the Victor/Victim model.

http://maketherightmovesbusinesscoaching.com/checkmatevideos/

ATTITUDE: TAKING RESPONSIBILITY

PROVE

[X] Proactive
[X] Responsible
[X] Ownership
[X] Visionary
[X] Excellence

VICTOR

Opportunity Seekers

Problems

BENDS

[X] Blame
[X] Excuses
[X] Negative
[X] Denial
[X] Scarcity

Failure Magnets

VICTIM

http://www.maketherightmovesbusinesscoaching.com/checkmatevideos

Victor/Victim Chart

People who live above the line have nothing to prove. They are comfortable in their own skin. They are proactive, they are responsible, they take ownership for all the decisions they make. They are visionary, forward thinking, focused, and they embrace personal and business excellence. These are the VICTORs of the world.

Those who live below the line bend with the trends. They blame others for frustrating situations and negative results. They have all sorts of excuses for why things are the way they are or the way they aren't. They are generally negative and exhibit a "Woe is me!" attitude. They live in a world of denial where there is no personal responsibility, no room for personal improvement, and no room for or value in the opinions and ideas of others. These are the VICTIMs of the world.

As a business owner or project manager, YOU are responsible. We all know people who operate above the line and people who operate below the line. You can't afford to be the victim. You need to be the VICTOR. YOU have the ability to take control and decide how you want to act or respond.

The Victor/Victim chart is a tool you can easily use with your team to help each individual understand the attitudinal and ethical expectations you have for them. The reality is that we can't always know what the project challenges may be or when they will present themselves to us. The uncertainty and spontaneity of challenges can elicit negative attitudes and behaviors, causing "below the line" activity. The key in guiding your team is to recognize when behavior starts to drop below the line and then do everything you can, scratch and claw if need be, to get back above the line.

Having the right attitude is critical for success. With your VICTOR mindset let's now focus on the process. Why do 80% of all technology ideas never come to fruition? Why do 80% of all construction projects fail to hit the scope schedule and target budget? Why are ideas so hard to implement? It is because people do not understand that learning and growth are essential for success. How many of your projects or ideas are carbon copies of the last? Not many. With each new endeavor, we must adapt, we must learn, we must stretch. There is a process we undergo as we take on a new project. It is delineated in the chart on the following page over four steps.

FOUR STEPS TO LEARNING: THE CONSCIOUSNESS/COMPETENCE CHART

Next, I've outlined the four steps to learning. The four steps to learning was an idea initially published by Noel Burch with Gordon Training International and is widely associated with Abraham Maslow, the father of Hierarchy of needs. These steps, when followed, will help you translate your ideas into results. I don't think much needs to be said here—the charts themselves should be wildly helpful! You're invited to visit the checkmate videos site (link below) to view a video presentation of the four steps to learning.

http://maketherightmovesbusinesscoaching.com/checkmatevideos/

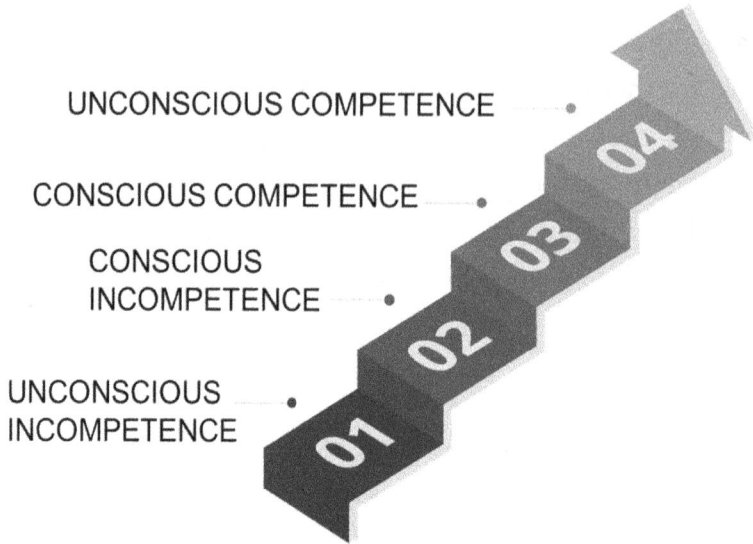

UNCONSCIOUS COMPETENCE

CONSCIOUS COMPETENCE

CONSCIOUS
INCOMPETENCE

UNCONSCIOUS
INCOMPETENCE

01 02 03 04

Consciousness/Competence Chart

Step #	Step Name	What this STEP Means	How to Move On to the Next Step (or not)
1	Unconscious Incompetence	Unconscious-lacking awareness Incompetence-lacking ability *I don't know what I don't know!*	Exposure and engagement with outside stimulus, new ideas, new information, new activity and the willingness to learn what is out there and how others do it. Be curious.
2	Conscious Incompetence	Conscious-aware Incompetence-lacking ability *I know what IT is, but I don't know HOW to do it.*	Evaluate the time, energy, and financial outlay and gains if you were to invest in learning the HOW. If it is worth it, will you or someone else on your team do the learning? Is there someone on your team who already knows the HOW?

| 3 | Conscious Competence | Conscious-aware Competent-Able

I am learning HOW to do it and understand its value to my project | Learn, practice, get feedback, reflect. Repeat cycle. |
| 4 | Unconscious Competence | Proficiency!

I know WHAT I need to do and I know HOW to do it. | Because your time is so valuable and time on tasks takes you away from other tasks, is this new knowledge and skill worthy of your time or better delegated to another member of the team or a new resource altogether? |

Let's look at a real life application to which we can all relate:

Riding a Bike

1- Conscious Incompetence	I don't know how to ride a bike.	I see people riding bikes. I want to join my friends who ride bikes. I don't want to rely on a driver to take me everywhere I want to go when they have time.
2- Conscious Incompetence	I want to ride a bike and I want to learn HOW.	It is definitely worth my time to learn because it will grant me some freedom to get to places when I want to go. It will also allow me to join my peer group in this activity. My dad knows how to ride a bike. I'll ask him if he can teach me!
3- Conscious Competence	My dad is teaching me how to ride a bike.	I learn how to get on and off the bike, how to steer, how to signal. I fall down. I get back on. My dad guides me as I practice. I want to keep doing this until I can do it on my own.
4- Unconscious Competence	I can ride a bike!	Now I want to drive a car!

1. **In Step 1, we don't know what we don't know.** You can't move off this step by yourself. You will need to learn what's out there and how others do it by exposing yourself to new information, new ideas, and new activities. This is the key component of the "Make the Right Moves" process. Once you are aware that something exists, you instantly transition to Step 2.

2. **In Step 2, we know the "what" but not the "how."** You are in control as you evaluate and decide if this is something of value to your project. If so, you'll move to Step 3. This is a place where you can make a decision to engage somebody else to do the work or learn it yourself.

3. **Step 3 requires us to learn, practice, and get feedback.** Again, if you think your priorities are higher in other areas, consider hiring or delegating this to someone else. Just because you know how to do something doesn't mean you are proficient. Accomplishing this step often requires practice and feedback.

4. **Step 4 is where we become proficient.** You have decided that investing time in new learning is beneficial to the success of the project.

So how do we use our knowledge of the Steps of the Consciousness/ Competence Process to take our ideas (Step 1) to yield results (Step 4) in the projects undertaken by our business? The desired outcome of many projects is to create income, to make money. These are deemed "offensive" projects. "Defensive" projects, such as compliance and safety projects, are designed to maintain what you already have. Whatever the motivation for the project, the process is the same for translating ideas into results.

Translating Ideas into Results

Translating ideas into money is a process.

IDEA – First you get an idea.

PRESENTATION – Then you need to present your idea to find a sponsor and to engage your team. Maybe it's just you. More frequently you need help from others – employees, service providers or stakeholders.

AGREEMENT – Then you need an agreement for performance and contribution.

SUCCESS – Success! Now you will see the result of all your hard work and efforts.

THE FIVE KEY ATTRIBUTES FOR TRANSLATING YOUR IDEAS INTO MONEY

TRANSLATING YOUR IDEA(S) INTO MONEY IS, AT IT'S MOST common definition, a project. A project has an end result, money, and a starting point, where you are today. Effectively managing the activities and tasks needed to move from the starting point to the ending point is the process for success. Listed below are five key attributes for any successful project. Starting with and following these five keys will eliminate and or minimize the most common time consuming and costly errors. Your insurance that these five keys are well addressed throughout the project will translate your ideas into your desired results more simply and easily. Money is the desired result for most ideas. Although not every idea. Money translates to time and financial freedom and it's rare that these two concepts don't headline the effort. If you make more money than you need you can help those that are less fortunate and leave a lasting legacy. This may be your end goal but money makes it far easier and is therefore a stepping stone to your legacy.

1. **Clarity—Clearly Defining the Problem or Opportunity and the Desired Result:**
   The greater the clarity with defining the issue and desired results, the greater the success.

2. **Sponsorship and Employee Engagement:**
   Sponsorship assigns financial ownership and responsibility to the project. Employee engagement refers to the team of people assigned to, invested in, benefitting in, and/or affected by the project. The sponsor is the leader and driver in the project and ultimately the key beneficiary of the project activity.

3. **Validating A Value Proposition:**
   There is never going to be enough time to do everything. There's only enough time to do the most important things. A validated value proposition provides you with a way to compare one idea to another or one opportunity to another, to clearly and objectively evaluate and prioritize activities.

4. **Action Plan:**
   The action plan that includes tasks, subtasks, timelines, resources, and milestones serves as your roadmap to success.

5. **Change Management Plan:**
   The change management plan is your roadmap through transition times. All plans are good only through the day they are completed. After that, they are subject to the changes that each day and week deliver. The change management plan is a systematic process for reviewing ideas, concepts, suggestions, and adversity in a manner that keeps the plan on course to achieve your desired results.

   Are you ready to begin? At the end of each key attribute section, you'll be asked to assess yourself (give yourself a grade on that key attribute) using the below Report Card model.

Your Current Report Card

Think about your high school or college report cards. The highest achievable grade was an A+. In business, your goal is to score an A+ on your projects and services. What grade would you give yourself now on current or past projects based on the Key Attributes? Let's see!

For the purposes of applying what you learn in this book to real life applications, choose a current or recent project, or a goal you are working on. Give yourself a grade for each Key Attribute—don't worry if you don't fully understand the attribute—we'll break it down later.

What is the project?

Now that you've identified the idea and the project, jot down what you believe is your current grade for each section.

1. A clearly defined problem and desired result?

2. Sponsorship and employee engagement?

3. A validated value proposition?

4. An action plan with resources and milestones?

5. A change management plan?

You're invited to visit my site (link below) to download a report card worksheet.

http://maketherightmovesbusinesscoaching.com/checkmateworksheets/

KEY ONE:
Clarity—Clearly Defining the
Problem or Opportunity and the
Desired Result

Clearly Defined Problem
and Result

"A problem clearly stated is a problem half solved."
—Dorothea Brande

Here are some questions to help you clarify the problem and desired results:

- WHY do we need to do X?
- WHAT specifically do we need to do?
- WHO will do it?
- WHEN will we do this?
- HOW do we do this? HOW MUCH will it cost?

When you provide effective answers to all of these questions, the project moves along at an efficient and focused pace. Larger more complex projects require greater depth and analysis to achieve clarity. The next section of this material will help you drill down even more by utilizing the SMART goal format. SMART goals are Specific, Measurable, Aligned with your values, Realistic, and Time bound.

Goal Setting with SMART Goals

In his book *Success Principles*, American author and motivational speaker Jack Canfield states, "In order for you to achieve a goal you must be very clear about what you want!" Using SMART goals will increase your chance of reaching and maintaining them by 1000%.

It is typical for us to create a list of **Specific** benefits for each project we take on. Why? Simple—the benefits reveal the focus or purpose of the project. The benefits provide us with *compelling* reasons to pursue the goal. Once we specify the goal, we need to create a system of **Measurements** to chart our progress toward the goal and decide if they are **aligned with our values.** Finally, we need to know that our goals are realistically capable of achieving the desired outcome and we need to develop a **Timeline** that maximizes the efficiency of the team and that takes into account the urgency of the project. SMART goals keep us accountable.

Time Bound

Realistic

Aligned with your values

Measurable

Specific

Note: For small business owners, staying aligned with their personal values accomplishes the relevancy factor and more. There is often a tremendous degree of energy needed to implement big ideas. Big, long-term, and highly valuable projects require a ton of time but can deliver huge value. Just think of some of the software projects or construction projects that you have been around or seen. They take years in the making. Now the other thing is that you have to be aligned with your values.

Being aligned with your personal values provides the energy and desire to persevere through the adversity that naturally occurs with change.

For you to have every advantage in order to implement your big idea, you need to make sure your goal is aligned with your core values. Today's values are often different than yesterday's. For example, "thinking green" (energy conservation) values are more relevant today than in the past. Your ideas need to fit into who you are, and be relevant. A solid strategy, as part of your goal setting exercise, is to spend some time identifying and understanding your core values and your life purpose to ensure that your ideas effectively support both. Use your value and life purpose definitions to support the goals you choose. Your business should support you and your life. Your life shouldn't support your business.

In and of themselves, goals and the accomplishment thereof, do not provide long term joy. Goals that are in harmony with the way we want to live—that help us or allow us to make the impact or contribution that we feel is important to others—provide the opportunity for long-term joy.

For more information on goal setting and SMART goals, you are invited to visit the checkmate videos site (link below) to view an extended Make the Right Moves Smart Goals video presentation.

http://maketherightmovesbusinesscoaching.com/checkmatevideos/

A note about timelines: Guidelines and deadlines for your goals provide compelling motivation for action. Setting schedules and deadlines engages your subconscious in the direction of your goal and helps you to identify solutions night and day. Timelines establish urgency around the activity. Urgency brings the action and the accomplishment front and center of your mental activity and drives solution oriented behavior.

The Ten (10) Goals Methodology (Or How to Write Goals)

The TEN Goals Methodology recommends writing at least ten business (or personal) goals each day. What matters most is that you focus on those things that you want instead of the things you do not want. Ralph Waldo Emerson wrote, "You become what you think about all day long." Hence, if you think about your goals, you achieve them. If you think about the impediments to your goals, you tend to be faced with more challenges. Successful people think about what they want and how to get it! In almost every case however, a second opinion is exceedingly valuable.

For a more detailed explanation on the value of a second set of eyes, you're invited to view the hidden opportunities video on the businesswhitt youtube channel.

https://www.youtube.com/watch?v=6HciTJ8GJq0&feature=youtu.be

SMART goal setting is a superb template for project development and personal goal planning. The following bullet points highlight some additional support for writing goals whether it be one or ten:

- Use "I" statements.

- Use positive language.

- Use present tense action verbs.

- Write out your goals on a daily basis.

Some good examples and poor examples to get you started:

Goal: Lose weight. (Current weight 210.)
Good Example: I weigh 200 pounds. (Positive affirmation of the goal.)
Poor Example: I want to lose ten pounds. (The word "lose" has a negative connotation.)

Goal: Quit smoking.
Good Example: I am free of nicotine. (Focus on the positive outcome.)
Poor Example: I do not smoke. (Use of a negative phrase.)

Goal: Increase financial status.
Good Example: I have a net worth of $1 million.
Poor Example: I need to make more money.

Don't forget that your goals need to be **SMART!**

Specific, Measurable, Aligned with your values, Realistic, and Time bound.

REPORT CARD TIME!

Go ahead and pull out the Report Card you filled out. Now that you know more about the first key attribute, **a clearly defined problem and desired result,** what grade would you give yourself?

Give yourself a high mark if you answered the who, what, where, why, when, how, and how much as it relates to your project.

If you can't answer some or all of these questions, your mark will be lower but now you can say, "These are the things I need to know and do to get an A+."

Project Charter at a Glance

Project Name: _____

Project Manager: _____

Project Sponsor: _____

Project Description:
[Use this space to describe the project at a high level.]

Project Background:
[Use this space to describe the situation that led to the need for this project. Look at business needs, user needs, and try to quantify challenges.]

Project Objective:
[Use this space to describe the specific results you expect to achieve for the business, your sponsor, and known stakeholder groups. The more measurable the better.]

Critical Success Factors:
[Use this space to describe the what has to happen in order for the project to be successful.]

Required Resources:
[Use this space to describe the required staffing for this project. If some resources are key, highlight them here as well.]

Constraints:
[Use this space to describe your assumptions and constraints that you must work within.]

Project Authority:
[Use this space to describe roles and responsibilities of each project participant and group. This section can also be presented in the form of a RACI matrix.]

ESSENTIAL TOOLS, KEY ONE

You're invited to visit the checkmate vides site (link below) to view a sample "Project Charter at a Glance" worksheet.

http://maketherightmovesbusinesscoaching.com/checkmateworksheets/

KEY TWO:
Sponsorship and
Employee Engagement

Sponsorship & Employee
Engagement

"You must capture and keep the heart of the original and supremely able man before his brain can do its best."
—Andrew Carnegie

Now that you have greater clarity on your project, we need to make sure that the right team is established. Rarely are ideas implemented with a team of one. Even if you are an employee of one, there are always others necessary to execute your idea including service providers and contractors. In the table below we've listed categories pertinent to all projects. Assign a person to every single category. In small businesses, the same individuals wear multiple hats. However, it is critical that every category is assigned a leader.

Roles and Responsibilities

Role	Responsibility	Name
Project Sponsorship	Policy Setting Funding Scope Management	
Project Guidance	Standards and Conventions Business Process Imperatives Change Management	
Project Control	Business Process Recommendations Issues Resolution Change Control	
Project Execution	Action / Activity Completion Training User Assimilation	

Project Sponsorship defines the person in charge of financing the project and making decisions involving policy, funding, and scope management.

Project Guidance defines the manager of the project who is adept at industry standards and conventions, and who guides the project along.

Project Control defines the person who ensures timelines and deadlines, and who makes recommendations regarding changes or issues surrounding the process.

Project Execution defines the person or people responsible for putting plans into action. Large companies may have one or more people identified for each role in this category.

For each of the roles in the Project Management Roles and Responsibilities chart, you'll want to answer some key questions about your team.

They are:

- **Who cares** (about this project) and **why?**
  Develop the list. This could be a few employees, or groups of employees, departments, department managers, Service providers, or others. Be sure to list out why.

- **What's the win?**
  What is the benefit from this project? The benefit might adjust depending on the list of who cares.

- **Who's going to play?**
  If people get to win, they want to play! Who wants to be on the team?

- **Who is going to make it work?**
  Who is needed to identify and implement the project? Who is available? Who has the will and the skill to effectively participate on the team?

One tool I use to answer some of these questions when I think about team roles and responsibilities is *Gleicher's Formula for Change*. The formula was created while he was working at Arthur D. Little in the early 1960s and is a model used to assess the strengths that affect the success of behavioral and organizational change in programs.

Ask yourself, "Are all my employees or team members on board from the get go of every project we take on?" Sometimes that answer is yes, sometimes maybe, and other times the answer is no. Using the Formula for Change is useful when we need to 1) get people involved, 2) ask them to change behavior, or 3) ask them operate differently from their current process. It is far more effective to have team members who feel engaged with the work and not forced into it.

Formula for Change

D x V x F x R

Dissatisfaction
with the status quo

First Steps
in the direction of the
vision

Vision
of positive possibility, more
that the absence of pain in the
present situation

Resistance
to change

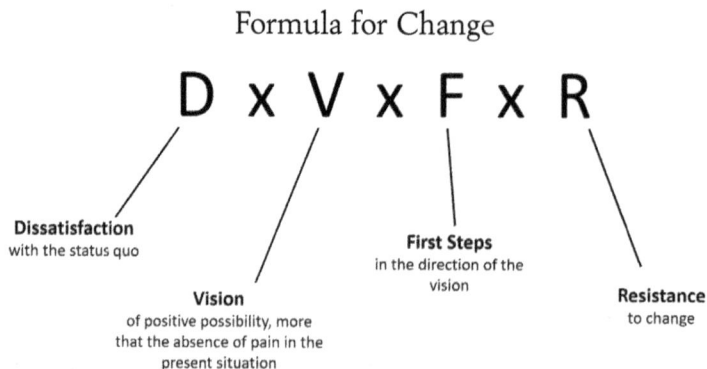

In 2005, Robert A. Gallagher explained the formula as described below. Its implications on behavioral and organizational change are far-reaching. You're invited to visit the checkmate videos site (link below) to view a video presentation of the Gliecher's formula.

http://maketherightmovesbusinesscoaching.com/checkmatevideos/

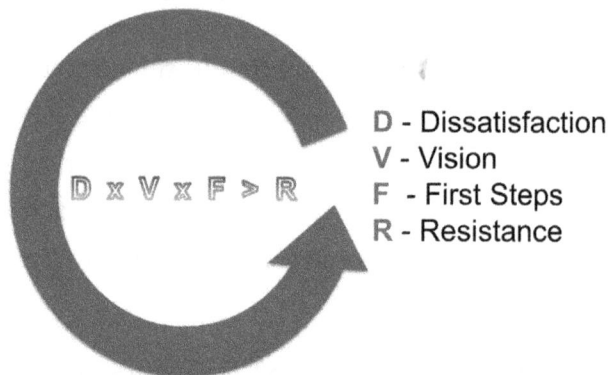

D x V x F > R

D - Dissatisfaction
V - Vision
F - First Steps
R - Resistance

1. Be **Dissatisfied (D)** with the way things are (in relationship to the proposed change).

2. Have a **Vision (V)**—an image or an idea of what improvement would look like, that is grounded in the hopes and dreams of employees or members. Just communicating the vision (or mission, or strategic plan) will not bring change.

3. Have a clear sense of what needs to be done as **First Steps (F)**. This means having a picture of what we can do differently in the short term that will move us toward that vision.

Four major factors for leaders to take into account are:

    1) What competencies need to be developed or strengthened for people to be able to function in the changed situation? People don't like to feel incompetent and change often creates that feeling.

    2) People are often hesitant to accept and implement the change because they fear losing friends and colleagues who are in opposition.

    3) Having the needed resources to make the change.

    4) Beginning to create an alignment of structures, processes, and practices that will be in harmony with the new way.

  4. *Last but not least,* **Resistance (R)** *is likely to be present in all change efforts. The combined weight of the dissatisfaction, vision, and first steps needs to be able to overcome this resistance.*

That means if any of those elements (D, V, F) is "0," the change will not be possible.

It is useful to use another theory here to apply this change formula. Chris Argyris's *Intervention Theory* suggests that the more people you get involved in diagnosing the situation, exploring options, and shaping a picture for the future, the more likely you are to develop a commitment in people that is sustainable under pressure and over time.

Are **you** prepared to take on behavioral and organizational change?

REPORT CARD TIME

Your Current Report Card

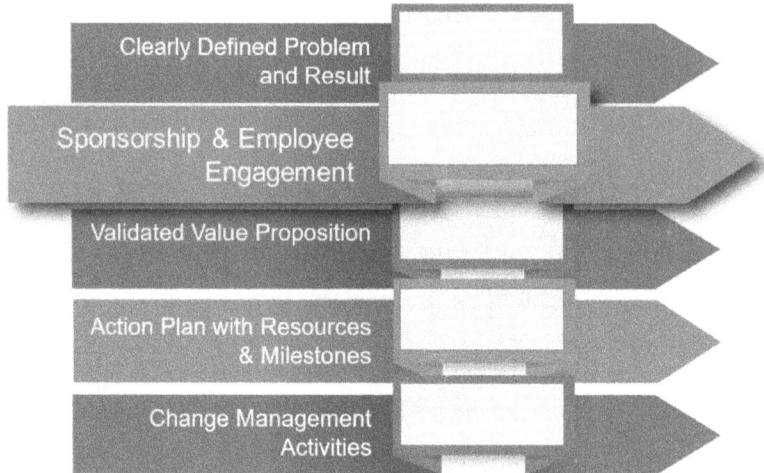

Clearly Defined Problem and Result	
Sponsorship & Employee Engagement	
Validated Value Proposition	
Action Plan with Resources & Milestones	
Change Management Activities	

Let's take a look back at your Report Card. Now that you know more about the second key attribute, **Sponsorship and Engagement**, what grade would you give yourself? Give yourself a high mark if you assigned an individual to each of the roles and if they are effectively engaged in the effort. If you can't answer some or all of these questions, your mark will be lower but now you can say, "These are the things I need to know and do to get an A+."

If you are not at an A+, you know that this is an area of growth for you and your business. You need to find the right people, get people more engaged, and get them to work together at maximum efficiency. This is your "X."

Change Request From

Business Whitt
by John Whitt

Project Name: _____   **Date:** _____

Project Manager: _____   **Change No:** _____

STANDARD CHANGE REQUEST TEMPLATE:

Change Category: [*Check all that apply*]

☐ Schedule   ☐ Cost   ☐ Scope   ☐ Requirements/Deliverables   ☐ Testing/Quality   ☐ Resources

Does this Change Affect: [*Check all that apply*]

☐ Corrective Action   ☐ Preventative Action   ☐ Defect Repair   ☐ Updates   ☐ Other

Describe the Change Being Requested:

Describe the Reason for the Change:

Describe all Alternatives Considered:

Describe any Technical Changes Required to Implement this Change:

Describe Risks to be Considered for this Change:

Estimate Resources and Costs Needed to Implement this Change:

Describe the Implications to Quality:

Disposition:

☐ Approve   ☐ Reject   ☐ Defer

Request Review Notes Approval, Rejection, or Deferral:

APPROVALS:

Name	Signature	Date

ESSENTIAL TOOLS, KEY TWO

You're invited to visit my website (link below) to view a sample "Sponsor-ship Chart" worksheet.

http://maketherightmovesbusinesscoaching.com/checkmateworksheets/

KEY THREE:
Validating the Value Proposition

Validated Value Proposition

"It's the little details that are vital. Little things
make big things happen."
—John Wooden

Now our focus turns deeper into project details:

- What will our project really **cost?** Time to uncover all of the rocks we can find.

- What will it actually **provide?** This is a deep dive into the benefits. How much money will it really make?

- How does it **compare** to other projects? Often ignored is competition from other opportunities.

- Who **agrees** with the assessment derived from the previous questions? Make sure you have your analysis reviewed by trusted sources.

If you are a small business owner, you may not need much more approval than yourself. However, ensuring your resources are effectively deployed on the most valuable activities is critical. In addition, you'll need to ensure that both your internal and external teams members are fully on board. Use your team to help fill out all of the deep details. In some instances, it may be wise to make an investment in a detailed feasibility study. It would be much better to make a small investment now to ensure a large mistake isn't made later.

Benefits vs Costs

With any project, it is important to outline your benefits and your costs. Consider the following:

Benefits

> *Operating cost reduction = saves money*

> *Increasing revenue = makes money*

> *Mitigating risk factors = prevents loss*

> *Increasing or maintaining employee satisfaction = attracts/retains customers*

> *Enabling corporate strategy = expansion, etc.*

Costs

✗ *Time vs Value calculations*

✗ *Complexity and Risk calculations (you may need additional capital for the project due to possible complexity and risk factors)*

✗ *One-time implementation costs*

✗ *New and/or on-going operating costs*

✗ *Deferral of other initiatives*

Now, how do you weigh the costs against the benefits? Georgia Perkey, Managing Partner with Inpoint Advisors shared this chart with me. It's amazingly simple and effective. I use this chart with virtually all of my clients with every significant investment decision. There are always new ideas and new projects that are added to the list. Every effort costs time or money or both and this simple chart is the decision tree. Using this chart, it's very simple to view your Return on Investment (ROI). The sample in the chart shows that Initiative 5 derived the highest ROI in terms of lower costs and higher benefits.

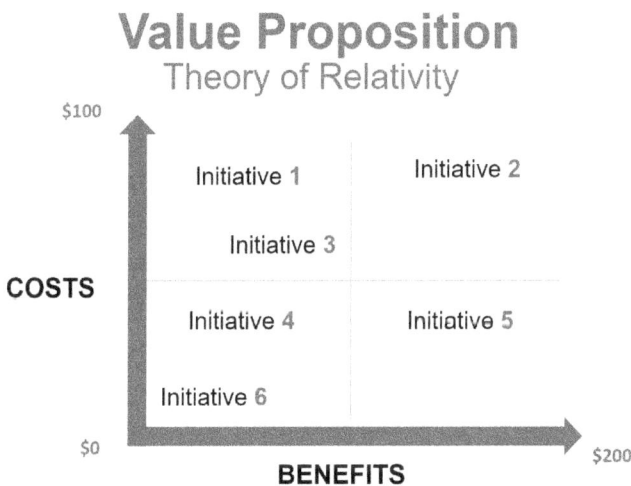

Value Proposition
Theory of Relativity

Value Proposition Chart

Let's assume that the bottom left corner of the chart represents $0, the top left arrow represents $100K, and the bottom right arrow equals $200K.

If you had to choose one project, what would it be? What about two projects? From the Chart, it looks like you might be able to accomplish initiatives 4, 5, and 6 for the same investment as initiative 2 and the results would be greater. Try doing this with your own initiatives! Think about your current or past projects/initiatives and their benefits and costs. Which project provided YOU with the highest ROI?

It's unusual for only one opportunity to be presented. Use this chart to help you compare multiple investment opportunities.

REPORT CARD TIME

Your Current Report Card

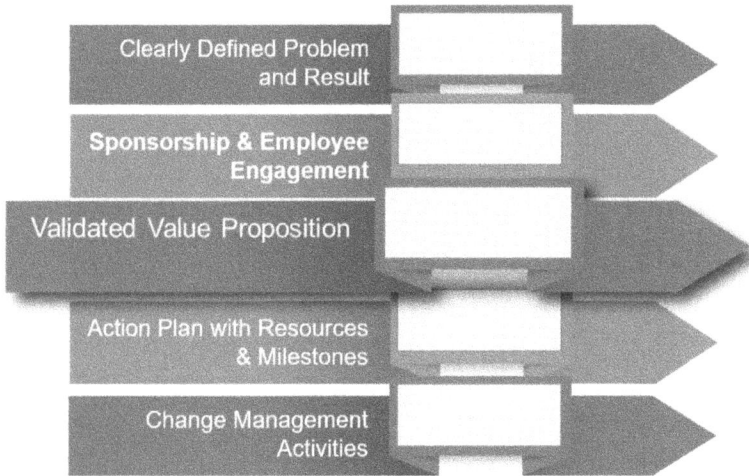

For many business owners, the Validated Value Proposition is something new and one that small business may not have adapted. Nevertheless, you'll need to re-assess yourself in this area. Now that you have a better understanding of the third key attribute, **a validated value proposition**, give yourself an updated grade. Have you been able to truly evaluate the costs and benefits of your initiatives? Give yourself an A+! If not, aim to identify the costs and benefits of your projects so that you will make the best decisions for a high ROI.

Value Proposition

Business Whitt
by John Whitt

THEORY OF RELATIVITY

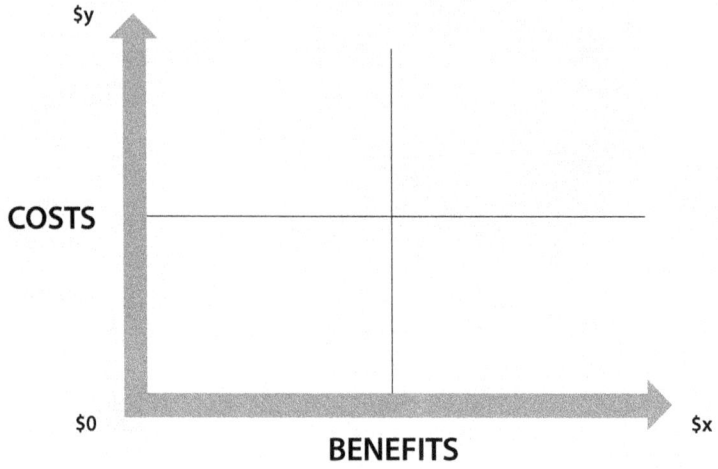

$y

COSTS

$0 $x

BENEFITS

	Benefit	Cost	ROI
Initiative #1			
Initiative #2			
Initiative #3			
Initiative #4			
Initiative #5			
Initiative #6			

ESSENTIAL TOOLS, KEY THREE

You're invited to visit my website (link below) to download a sample validated value proposition chart.

http://maketherightmovesbusinesscoaching.com/checkmateworksheets/

KEY FOUR:
Action Plan With Resources & Milestones

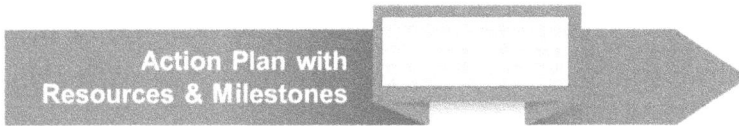

Action Plan with Resources & Milestones

"A goal without a plan is just a wish."
—Antoine de Saint-Exupéry

How good is your project planning? Now that you've identified the highest value initiatives, ask yourself these questions:

- What's my *approach?*
- What's my *plan?*
- What *resources* do I need?
- What's my *timeline?*
- How will this be *managed?*
- How will progress and issues be *communicated?*

A key in project management is the **how? How** will this be managed? **How** will we communicate along the way? **How** will we mobilize our team to move ahead?

Previously, we've looked at Defining the Problem, the Sponsorship and Engagement, and Validating the Value Proposition. These are all design activities and happen at the *beginning* of a project, at a time when you are not spending a lot of money. As the project proceeds, more and more dollars are accumulated against the effort. Changes in the early stages of the project are relatively less costly. Changes late in the process can be significant. In a construction project example the project cost per day jumps dramatically once construction starts. The point of implementation is when you begin to accrue higher costs and costs increase as the project continues. Quality action planning streamlines resources and resource costs and minimizes the cost of change. Any change late in the project may create a rework scenario of work that had previously been completed.

Accelerate the worry curve to reduce the cost of change. In the following chart, we're showing an important concept called accelerating the cost of change. In the early stages of a project, few resources are committed. You can see from the chart that the cost of change at this point in a project is relatively low. However, once we begin to implement, the cost of change skyrockets. For example, it's easier to make a change to a floor layer of a building in the design change. However, changing the plan while in the middle of construction may require tear down, rebuilds, and a possible loss of materials.

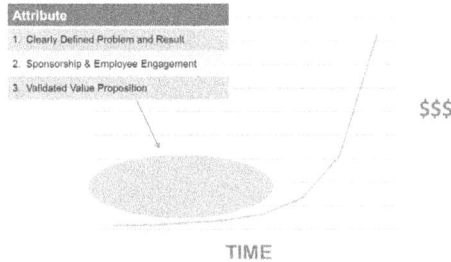

The cost of change continues to accelerate into the later stages of a project. This is why planning is so important. It's designed to minimize *late stage 'crazy expensive' change.*

Three Eyes of the Business Owner

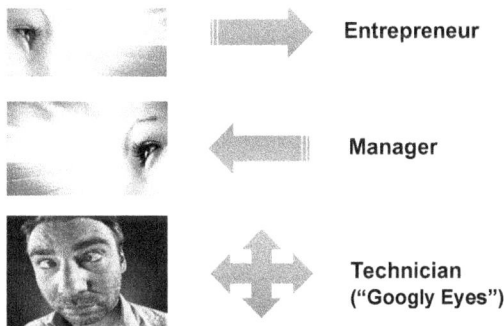

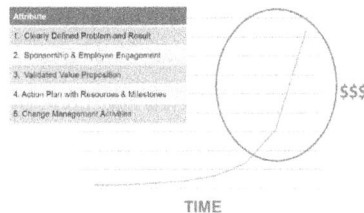

You're invited to visit the checkmate videos site (link below) to view a video presentation of the Three Eyes of the Entrepreneur model.

http://maketherightmovesbusinesscoaching.com/checkmatevideos/

In your Action Planning, consider FocalPoint's *Three Eyes of the Business Owner* principle. This was introduced by entrepreneur, small business leader, and author of *The E-Myth Revisited*, Michael Gerber. Gerber says that there are three perspectives within each business owner—that of entrepreneur, manager, and technician. Most businesses fail, or fail to move beyond a lifestyle business, because they are run by "technicians" with limited business skills. Many business owners are working "in the business" (technician)…rather than "on the business" (entrepreneur).

Some notable differences between the roles as cited by Gerber are described in the chart below.

Entrepreneur	Technician ("Googly Eyes")
Asks, "How must my business work?" *The business is the product and the key to success.*	Asks, "What work has to be done?" *The product cost, features, and support are the key to success.*
Sees the business as a system.	Sees the business as a place where people work.
Has a well-defined vision, matching projects to that vision.	Begins with the project uncertain of the future and vision.

The Entrepreneur is outwardly focused and asks questions like what if and how could we…. This is the role where products and services are designed and created. The Manager role is more inwardly focused and asks different questions like How much and when and how many. The Technician role is focused on the details. Are you balanced effectively or trapped in the weeds with Googly Eyes? Are you all over the place—thinking, doing, fixing…?

Maintaining a balance of views is what makes the manager perspective an essential part of the equation. The manager will help to build the processes and systems inherent to the project. This is where efficiency is highlighted.

Your biggest ROI will come from the time you spend in the entrepreneurial realm. This takes planning! Review your project charter. Review your roles and responsibilities. Where can you and your talents add the most value? Where does it make sense to engage other professionals or resources? Maximizing your time and your teams efficiency has a dramatic impact on ROI.

Building the Work Plan

Let's start to build the Action plan. There are three key factors to consider in this:

1. Tasks / Action Items

    • Identify your tasks and action items.

    • Define your Major Task Categories and assign each task to a category. You may find you have sub-categories depending on the size of your project.

2. Timing

    • Define the length of time required to complete each activity/task.

    • Identify and assign due dates for deliverables.

3. Resources

    • Define the resources needed to complete each task.

The more accurate you are with the Task/Action Items, the more accurate your timing and resources will be. Be sure to include key team members to help you identify the Tasks /Action Items.

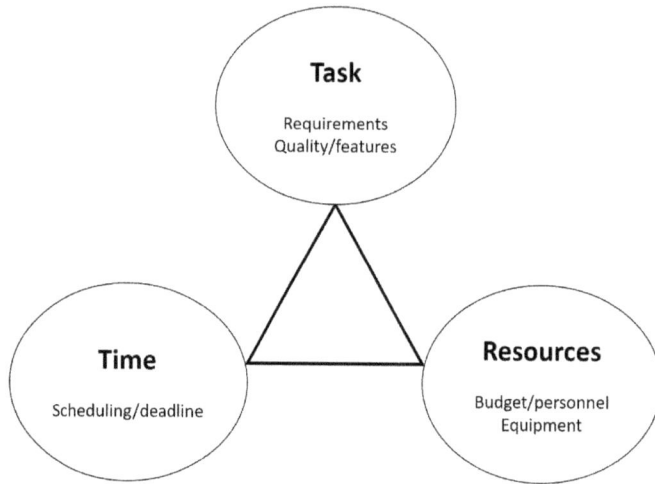

"The Golden Triangle"

Here's an example of what planning for an event might look like as divided into our key components of task, time and resources.

Task / Subtasks	Time to Complete	Start On	End On	Resource 1	Resource 2	Resource Total
Invitations				1	1	2
Create guest list						
Design invitation						
Mail invitations						
Manage RSVPs						
Budget				0.5	0	0.5
Create budget						
Manage expenses						
Food				4	4	8
Plan menu						
Cook food						
Serve food						
Room & Equipment				1	3	4
Pick Site / Room						
Order Tables/Chairs						
Make Decorations						
Set up Room						
Conclusion				2	1	3
Customer gifts						
Customer feedback						
Results						

Note the **Major Tasks** versus the **sub-tasks**.

Once Tasks are defined, developing a timeline is the next step. As you look at the table above, you'll note that some of the tasks are interdependent and/or require one task to be complete before another is started. Allotting the proper amount of time on each task and identifying task dependencies streamlines your project. Engage your project team to help identify the tasks, resources and dependencies necessary to fulfill the task. Lastly, you'll need to define the Milestones to mark those critical junctures in your plan. For smaller projects a simple spreadsheet may be all that is necessary to manage a project plan. Consider technological solutions for more complex projects where the number of tasks and dependencies are significant. The bottom line is … you need a plan.

REPORT CARD TIME

Your Current Report Card

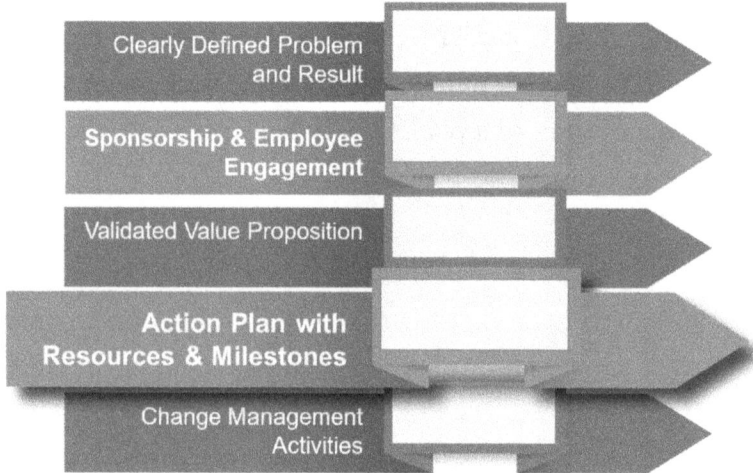

Clearly Defined Problem and Result	
Sponsorship & Employee Engagement	
Validated Value Proposition	
Action Plan with Resources & Milestones	
Change Management Activities	

It's time to rate yourself on the fourth key attribute, **action plan with resources & milestones**. Many small business owners have much room for improvement in this area, so don't be disappointed if your score is low at this time. When you begin to implement ideas from *Make the Right Moves* and follow the models provided, your increased skill and confidence to execute a project will raise your rating in this area.

Time Line Project Plan Worksheet

Business
Whitt
by John Whitt

Project Name: _____

Project Manager: _____

Project Sponsor: _____

No.	Tasks/Subtasks	Days to Complete	Start Date	Complete	Resource 1	Resource 2	Total Resources	Milestones

ESSENTIAL TOOLS, KEY FOUR

You're invited to visit my site (link below) to download a sample action plan worksheet.

http://maketherightmovesbusinesscoaching.com/checkmateworksheets/

KEY FIVE:
Change Management Plan

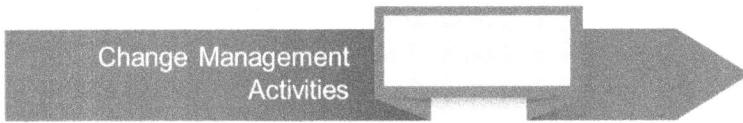

*"The **rate of change** is not going to slow down anytime soon.
If anything, competition in most industries will probably
speed up even more in the next few decades."*
—John P. Kotter

It is inevitable that we will encounter changes in the scope of any project and therefore we need a plan for handling changes and change requests? What kinds of changes are needed? How do you handle change? How does your team handle change?

Successful transition occurs when people feel valued and cared about. "People don't care about your products and service until they know you care." Consider all of your shareholders in the change management process. ALL changes impact the "Golden Triangle" of tasks, time, and resources. By taking into account the ideas, input, opinions, and needs of your team, you will enhance their collaboration, and increase production. You must analyze and evaluate changes from the three perspectives of the "Golden Triangle." Pick and choose wisely. Each change will have a cost and a benefit. Remember that the cost of change accelerates as the projects move closer to completion.

Pareto's Principle – The 80/20 Rule

Pareto's Principle is a useful approach when considering change decisions for your project(s). Leveraging and managing your resources effectively is the key to success and you need to make decisions that reap the greatest ROI. Italian economist Vilfedo Pareto described an unequal relationship between inputs and outputs. His principle stated that 20% of the invested input is responsible for 80% of the results obtained.

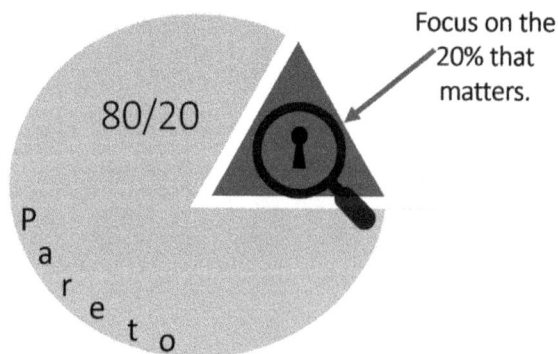

You're invited to visit the checkmate videos site (link below) to view a video presentation of the Pareto Principle model.

http://maketherightmovesbusinesscoaching.com/checkmatevideos/

Doesn't it make sense to focus on the top 20% of activities that bring 80% of the results? You can get mired in minutiae or you can decide to stay focused on the most important and valuable components for your project. You can use the validated value proposition to determine which changes (if any) have the highest ROI. When considering various opportunities for change ask yourself—what should I stop doing? What should I start doing? How much of the actual work should I be performing?

Once you've defined or accepted any changes to the plan you need to communicate to your project stakeholders. This is the list you defined in the "Engaging roles and responsibilities" chapter. Regular communication on how the project is proceeding and project changes are critical to retaining project engagement. Identify what this will look like. Is this a simple e-mail distribution? Should it be distributed in an employee or customer newsletter? How frequently should you communicate the information? A quality change management plan includes decisions and communication.

REPORT CARD TIME

Your Current Report Card

Clearly Defined Problem and Result

Sponsorship & Employee Engagement

Validated Value Proposition

Action Plan with Resources & Milestones

Change Management Activities

Take a look back at your first Report Card to the "Change Management Activities" section. Did you write anything in that box at all? If so, has your score changed? If not, will it be different for the next project? Go ahead and grade yourself on the final, fifth key attribute, **change management plan**.

Now that you've explored the five key attributes on your Report Card you are ready to take on your next project. Make a habit of completing your report card at the beginning of each project. These five key attributes will enhance your success and minimize headaches for all of your projects.

Project Status Report

Business
Whitt
by John Whitt

Project Name: _____

Project Manager: _____

PROJECT STATUS SUMMARY

Percent Complete: _____ %

Scope	Schedule	Cost	Risks	Quality

This section provides a quick executive overview of the status of the project. It is intended for high level management so it should not get too much into the details of the project. However, it should highlight anything specific which should be brought to their attention. The Scope/Schedule/Cost/Quality table above is a quick way to present a color coded dashboard for the status report. Typically a variance of +/- 5% will warrant a yellow cautionary color and +/- 10% will warrant a red warning color. For a project which needs tighter control +/- 2% and +/- 5% are used for these thresholds; whereas, other projects with less strict control may use 10% and 20% variances. The percent complete here should be the percent completion of the entire project. For any constraint which is yellow or red this section should contain brief explanation the reason why.

EXAMPLE : The project schedule is 7% behind schedule due to inclement weather which has affected the installation of the fiber optics throughout the campus. This should not affect the project completion date as crews are planning to make up the time by working weekends and extended hours next month.

EXAMPLE: The project risks is red due to the inclement weather and servers which were delivered last month weren't configured with the correct hardware specifications. The impact of the inclement weather on the schedule will be mitigated by having crews make up the time by working weekends and extended hours next month. Currently we are working with the server vendor to resolve the server hardware configuration problem. The configuration delivered will not handle the work load of going live in two months; however, it is sufficient for development and testing activities scheduled prior to going live.

Now fill in your own project below:

WORK PLANNED FOR LAST WEEK

For this section you can copy the "Worked Planned for Next Week" section from last week's status report and paste it into this section.

WORK COMPLETED LAST WEEK

In this section you should provide a highlight of work performed and milestones and/or deliverables met during the past week.

WORK PLANNED FOR NEXT WEEK

Provide an overview of the work being performed during the next week and any milestones or deliverables you expect to meet.

OPEN ISSUES

This section should contain a list of open issues along with their status.

OPEN RISKS

This section should contain a list of all open risks (risks which have occurred, or are on the verge of occurring).

DELIVERABLES AND MILESTONES

This section is a quick table which shows the status of the project milestones and deliverables.

The first column is for the name of the Milestone or Deliverable as it's in the project plan. The next column is the WBS number, this makes it easier to find the milestone/deliverable in the project plan. Planned is the planned date according to the approved project plan, the forecasted is the date you expect and actual is the actual date the milestone was met or deliverable was delivered. The status is a simple one or two word status such as; completed, on schedule, behind schedule, accepted, etc.

Milestone	WBS	Planned	Forecasted	Actual	Status
Deliverable	WBS	Planned	Forecasted	Actual	Status

OPEN CHANGE REQUESTS

Use this section to track all changes to the project and report the status of those changes. Tracking of changes starts with the request for the change, tracks the approval status and ends when the change is added to the project, the project plan and schedule update and it has become a part of the project.

Change Request Name	Change Request Number	Request Date	Current Status

KEY PERFORMANCE INDICATORS (KPI's)

Many managers turn right to this section as it provide a clear view of the status of the project according the earned value metrics. In your project you need to decide which metrics to monitor, but be sure not to include too many as you may end up providing the same information but in different forms. We like to track SV, SPI, CV and CPI in the layout below. Next to the schedule and cost headings you should state whether the project is ahead of or behind schedule and over or under budget. Notice we left out the word on - it is highly unlikely that you. If you like you can also include a paragraph at the beginning of this section presenting the earned value results in verbose.

Schedule - Project is *Ahead of/Behind* Schedule

Schedule Variance (SV): $ _____

Schedule Performance Index (SPI):   _____

Cost - Project is *Over/Under* Budget

Cost Variance (CV): $ _____

Cost Performance Index (CPI):   _____

ESSENTIAL TOOLS, KEY FIVE

You're invited to visit my site (link below) to download a sample Change Request Form and Project Status Report.

http://maketherightmovesbusinesscoaching.com/checkmateworksheets/

FINAL THOUGHTS:
A REVIEW OF THE KEY PRINCIPLES

IN EACH OF THE KEY ATTRIBUTES, I MAKE MENTION OF A principle that applies to that particular key. Below, I've summarized the main idea of that principle so you can easily reference it here.

Icon	Principle	Main Idea
	Victor vs Victim	The right attitude makes all the difference to your project.
	Four Stages of Learning	You need to position yourself for success by asking the to know your location on the learning curve.
	SMART Goal Setting	SMART goals are **S**pecific, **M**easurable, **A**ligned with your values, **R**ealistic, and **T**ime bound.
$D \times V \times F > R$	**Gleicher's Formula**	A win-win formula for engaging your team.
	The Eyes of the Business Owner	Make the best use of your time to get the greatest ROI.

| | **The 80/20 Rule** | The right focus = the greatest results. |

You're invited to visit the checkmate videos site to view a video presentation on each of these principles

http://maketherightmovesbusinesscoaching.com/checkmatevideos/

BONUS SECTION
THE LIFE CYCLE OF A BUSINESS: THE SIGMOID CURVE

*"The flower that wilted last year is gone. Petals once fallen
are fallen forever. Flowers do not return in the spring, rather
they are replaced. It is in this difference between returned and
replaced that the price of renewal is paid."*
—Daniel Abraham, The Price of Spring

CONGRATULATIONS! YOU'VE FINISHED MY BOOK. WELL,
almost. I am including one final section—I'm calling it a "bonus" section.
You certainly could just read through the five key attributes of a successful
project and end there, moving through each one with your idea or project
in mind, and working to bring it to the finish line.

But, maybe you have too many ideas floating around and you just aren't
sure which one to pursue. The five key principles were written assuming
you already have a project or an idea that you can take through the five
key attributes. Without that idea, you can't execute anything and you
can't move forward.

So, it's time to identify which idea, or what kind of idea, you should follow. This bonus section will help you do that. This will help you to identify where your business is currently in the business lifecycle and what to look for or accomplish in the next step and you can watch out for certain traps, or hang-ups, that have frustrated or ruined business for years.

Identifying where your business is positioned in the "Life Cycle of a Business" chart is helpful in determining the types of projects that should be considered when pushing forward.

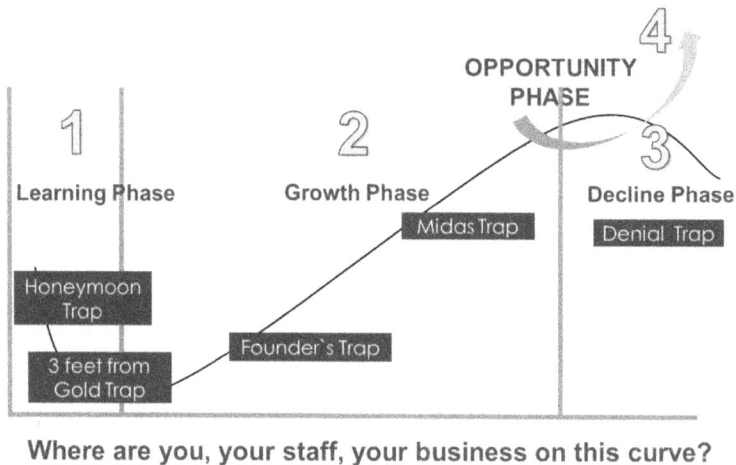

Where are you, your staff, your business on this curve?

Over time, business has several definable phases:

    1—Learning

    2—Growth

    3—Declining

    4—Opportunity

Phase 1, the Learning Phase, is essentially start-up. Learning your market, learning your customers, fine tuning products, etc. Phase 2, the Growth Phase generally means consistent recurring revenue from a common set of products and services. Phase 3, the Decline Phase occurs when new products come on the market that compete with our own or your own products and services become outdated due to technology or differentiated services.

Some caveats for you—in the Learning Phase, a business owner can experience a euphoria akin to a Honeymoon Phase when he's had some initial success. Sometimes, sudden success lulls us into the ***Honeymoon Trap***. This is not the time for over-the-top celebrations. Remember the Internet and the start of the dot.com industry? Many folks celebrated their initial success in lavish style only to be out of business before long. Here today, gone tomorrow. With this initial success, take the time to invest in yourself by putting some of your returns into reserve. Your reserve is there to support the inevitable and often surprising changes in the market place.

Another trap that catches new or early business owners is called **3 *Feet from Gold***. There are hundreds, thousands, and millions of great ideas that never come to fruition because the owner decides to give up, quit, and move in another direction. If your plan or idea is sound (tested), then it is simply a matter of identifying all of the solutions. It may take some time and it may take some resources but quitting is not the answer. You may need to adjust the plan via the change management process and this happens all the time but the project isn't scrapped unless the validation models are proven to be inaccurate and it no longer meets the objective. We see business owners start down a path and shift and shift and shift and they never get anything completed. Then they run out of resources and have to get a job. Persevere! Running a business isn't for the faint of heart. Perseverance is a top quality in successful business owners. Refuse to give up. But you need to feel confident that this idea, product, or service is sure to deliver big value in the marketplace. Translating ideas into results is designed to help you break through this trap. Better systems and planning will complete the project faster with fewer resources.

The Make The Right Moves Program is designed to help you break through this trap. There is a tremendous degree of learning needed for the new business owner. Understand that. Arrange to secure the help you need to make sure you get through that trap.

You'll know when you've broken through the Three Feet From Gold Trap when you have consistent cash flow. The business has a consistent repeatable process that generates opportunities and customers. It's hard to get to this state. It often requires immense effort. In the beginning, the business owner frequently has more time than money. This means that if you want something done, you do it yourself. It's called "sweat equity" and is used to describe how most successful small business are created. Long hours designing, implementing, marketing, and selling your products and services are required to get to consistent, repeatable cash flow. Once you have that consistent cash flow, you have transitioned to the growth phase and you can begin to move up the revenue curve.

The first trap you'll encounter in the growth phase is called the **Founder's Trap**. This is where sweat equity meets the end of the road. At some point there is simply not enough time to continue doing it yourself.

If you have to do it all yourself, you get stuck at this phase of business building because there is only so much time in a day. It is the single most limiting factor that every business owner must face. This is the technician trap. Where the business owner can find themselves so deep into the business that the idea of working on the business is just too far fetched. This is a growth stopping point for many. The learning curve has to shift from designing and implementing to leveraging.

The key to this trap is leverage. The projects at this stage are designed to leverage cash, employees, and equipment to expand the business.

Whether or not you decide to grow your business into a regional or national powerhouse or not, the **Midas Trap** is lurking throughout the Growth Phrase. It's called the Midas Trap because successful business owners can get lulled into a false sense of security aka thinking irrationally that the results will continue on forever. The reality is that this just doesn't happen. Life changes, markets change, competitors arise. The key to avoiding this trap is not to take your eyes off the ball. In this phase, it's about implementing a system that watches and looks and learns all the time. A system that keeps you ahead of the curve. Market research, customer engagement, and innovation lead the charge. Take your eyes off the ball at your own risk. There are plenty of companies that have experienced this tragedy. Then the down-curve happens. Dominant industries have fallen from this trap.

Our last trap is called the **Denial Trap**, part of the Decline Phase. Businesses rarely fail over night. At first, the downturn is often quite gradual. Results are just a bit less than expected. Quarterly results fall a bit short and growth flattens out. Failure to heed these warning signs and the rest can snowball quickly. Vigilance is the key. When results start to disappear, you must investigate. And the earlier the better. Catch a market shift or a competitive shift early and launch into Phase 4 new opportunities. This is where projects for re-invention and innovation are critical. You have a choice to be the Victor or the Victim here. The Victor creates the positive change necessary to keep the business moving.

Identify where you and your staff are on the sigmoid curve graph and you can start your project process more effectively. This simple exercise will help identify the types of projects that are likely to propel your business to the next level.

Build your rainy day reserve, bust through the Three Feet from Gold Trap, stay in the Growth Phase and away from the Decline Stage. You're invited to visit the checkmate videos site (link below) view a video presentation on the sigmoid curve.

http://maketherightmovesbusinesscoaching.com/checkmatevideos/

Constant and continuous positive change will keep you on the path to success. As a final concept to iterate the value of a continuous improvement, consider the 1% Rule, which argues that constant and continuous incremental change produces massive results over time. This is the power of compound interest. As Albert Einstein famously said, "Compound interest is the most powerful force in the universe."

You're invited to view an extended video on the 1% Rule here:

https://www.youtube.com/watch?v=-zBPrgDtqpQ&feature=youtu.be

ABOUT THE AUTHOR

JOHN WHITT HAS BEEN IN THE COACHING practice one way or the other for over sixteen years. For the last six and a half years, John has been a part of the FocalPoint Coaching team, which is powered by Brian Tracy.

John identifies himself as a "DIY guy." Growing up with wrenches, hammers, screwdrivers, drills, lathes, etc., he learned to use tools to create tools. While most people pay someone else to fix something, John is comfortable fixing, creating, and building it all himself. Realizing how comfortable he is with change, he realized he wasn't like most people. It was this discovery that led John to get into coaching and working with people to create change.

The reason John believes most business fail is that they don't know how to fix their problems. Folded into that is that they can't seem to make the right moves to even begin the fixing process. As a result, they find themselves trying to work **ON** their own business when they are really working **IN** their business. And while they may be working hard, they are not making any progress—they stay static or even worse, start going backwards. Whether they realize it or not, they've abandoned business dreams and growth while they are out trying to make money for that same business.

With thirty years of corporate experience building businesses as large as $500MM annually, a continuous improvement mindset, good intuition and a comfort level with risk, and the proper training and tools from Brian Tracy, John Whitt will take chaos and create smooth and streamlined results.

The best of the best are always learning and growing. Life is a downward escalator and if you're not going up, you're going down. There is no static.

Join John as he will provide you with the tools, information, knowledge, and techniques to run a successful small business. Commit yourself to finding joy in the process, and profiting in continuous upward growth.

CLARITY AT A GLANCE WORKSHEET

The next page shows you a sample Clarity At A Glance worksheet. Please visit my site (link below) to download samples of all the worksheets mentioned in this book, or to purchase a set of blank worksheets, which you can fill out anytime you have a project you'd like to complete.

http://maketherightmovesbusinesscoaching.com/checkmateworksheets/

Project Clarity Charter at a Glance

Project Name:	Expansion Services
Project Manager:	John Whitt
Project Sponsor:	Dr. Sample

Project Description:
Company founder: Dr. Sample believes significant expansion opportunities exist for the Company service line. Their services are one of the most profitable service lines at Company, with an average profit margin of 40%. The annual gross revenue opportunity range is $420K-$900K.

Project Background:
Company currently services the legal community and averages 25 clients per month. Each client is valued between $1000 and $1500 for each service instance. Current marketing spend is $1700/month.

Project Objective:
Increase ABC Service line opportunities by 35-50 opportunities per month using digital marketing. Annual revenue target $420-$900K.

Critical Success Factors:
Several critical success factors are associated with this project:
1. Linked in relationship building
2. Email list building purchase and development
3. Content marketing strategy development and implementation
4. Explainer video and explainer video search engine optimization
5. Website re-build
6. Online Rapport building conversion training
7. Strategic alliance partnership model development

Required Resources:
BusinessWhitt, Marketing Service co, Internal resources.

Constraints:
1. Project Budget: Recurring Project budget estimate is approximately $4200/Month
     a. Year 1: $50,400
     b. Year 2-5: $24,000
2. One-time expense estimate: $3000
     a. Annual Web updates: $5000
3. One time explainer video and SEO for explainer video: $1000
4. Content Marketing Material: TBD
5. Scope: to be finalized
6. Schedule: to be finalized

Project Authority:
Dr. Sample

www.ingramcontent.com/pod-product-compliance
Lightning Source LLC
Chambersburg PA
CBHW081824200326
41597CB00023B/4380